Leading with Science

The Logic of Team Leadership:

How Teams are Formed, Managed, and Maintained

by Martina Sprague

Copyright 2013 Martina Sprague

All rights reserved. No part of this text may be reproduced in any form or by any means, electronic or otherwise, without the prior written permission of the author.

Acknowledgement:

Back cover image pictures Knowledge Management Framework, which comprises a range of strategies and practices used to identify, distribute, and enable adoption of insights and experiences. Image source: Binesh Jose, reproduced under Wikimedia Commons license.

TABLE OF CONTENTS

Introduction	4
A Lesson in Logic and Truth	7
The Scientific Method	16
One Size Does Not Fit All	22
Who Stole "I" From Team?	27
Team versus Individual Excellence	35
Ways to Lead with Science	41
What Do You Owe Your Team?	55
Constructive Criticism? Oh Yeah?!	57
The End or the Means?	61
Evaluating the Leader	64
My Team Leader	70
Can You Hear the Talk?	76
Notes	85

INTRODUCTION

Although leadership books and popular slogans such as, "today is the first day of the rest of your life," or "half-full is better than half-empty," can aid thinking, when reality contradicts theory, you should go with reality. Reality in leadership is often what your gut tells you and not what you wish for, nor what some mathematical equation or scientific principle suggests. The logic of leadership is grounded in empirical evidence of right or wrong behavior, and, yes, the leader must face a level of personal risk. A leader who is so passionate about an idea that it brings him to tears may momentarily touch some hearts, but he will rarely win the minds of his team without demonstrating the will to inconvenience himself for his cause. Moreover, successful leadership requires a holistic approach supported by innovative ideas. Knowing how to think rather than what to think may be the leader's greatest asset. Knowing how to think involves a conscious element of skepticism. It requires awareness of biases related to previous experiences, strong personal views, or current ambitions.

This book explores the strengths and weaknesses of team leadership from a scientific/logic perspective and analyzes different ways to Lead with Science. It breaks down the parts that make up a team, and demonstrates elusive concepts such as why the team is not for everybody, and why there is in fact an "I" in team. It discusses logic argumentation, the importance of using proper definitions when communicating, and getting the employees to agree with the premises. It also debunks common motivational ideas and explores factors that increase motivation. It ends by recognizing the selfish needs of the team, and demonstrates how to achieve positive results when critiquing and evaluating performance.

The material in this book is excerpted from the previously published book, *Leadership, It Ain't Rocket Science: A Critical Analysis of Moving with the Cheese and Other Motivational Leadership Bullshit*, also by Martina Sprague.

> "The important thing in science is not so much to obtain new facts as to discover new ways of thinking about them."
>
> — Sir William Bragg

> "Every great scientific truth goes through three stages. First, people say it conflicts with the Bible; next, they say it has been discovered before; lastly, they say they always believed it."
>
> — Louis Agassiz

> "For we study strategy as a science: the application of that knowledge is an art."
>
> — Colonel Ned B. Rehkopf

A LESSON IN LOGIC AND TRUTH

Science is fascinating not because of the discoveries but because of the predictability; finding that the truth is in fact logic and steadfast, and that the concepts that were true a thousand years ago and earlier are still true today and most likely will be true tomorrow.[1] The leader who knows the truth and sees the evidence will have no problem foregoing debate and accepting the conclusion. He or she can enjoy the benefit of doing things right from the beginning. By contrast, the leader who fails to use science and logic to convince his or her team of a particular problem will come across as unintelligent or irrational. He or she will risk creating a chain reaction of strategic mistakes that may take years to fix, or that cannot be fixed.

Science involves the discovery of evidence and relationships; it demonstrates why things work the way they do. Technology gives us the tools and procedures. Science gives us a clear field of vision. Technology allows us to pursue our goals without second-guessing the outcome of our actions. Scientific principles used as analogies for leadership can teach a number of important concepts. For example, in the physical sciences a wave is defined as the transfer of energy from the source to a distant receiver. Wave motion can reveal something about the source: If a stone is dropped into a pond of water, waves will travel outward in expanding circles. But if two stones are dropped into the water, the waves produced by each stone can overlap and form an interference pattern. Within this pattern, wave effects may increase, decrease, or be neutralized. In other words, the two wave patterns can create a mutual reinforcement in some areas and a cancellation in others. When the crest of one wave overlaps the crest of another, the individual effects are added and called *constructive interference*. A leadership analogy can now be created: The two waves have "team worked" and produced an overall stronger wave.

The term *constructive* can be misleading, however. In the conceptual sense, an overall stronger "wave" does not necessarily translate into an overall more positive or efficient workforce. Depending on the circumstances and on what one is trying to achieve, *destructive interference*, where the disturbance is minimized and the wave pattern flattened may, in fact, have a more constructive effect in the work environment. The careful observer, whether supervisor or employee, will do himself and the team a service by carefully analyzing how he applies scientific analogies to team leadership.

One definition of *science* is knowledge that has been derived from direct observation and experimentation. Based on that knowledge, a number of principles are formed. But to truly form a rational opinion of the usefulness of science as a leadership tool, ask: What kind of knowledge, and studied for what purpose? How were the observations and experiments conducted? What is meant by principles? What is leadership, anyway? *What if* the leader relies on science to encourage cooperation and construct a desirable outcome, but really has no idea where he is going?

The danger with Leading with Science is that the use of scientific principles presupposes a leadership style that is based on specific techniques and thus remains unaltered by innovation. The fundamental principle of logic states that if the premises (the examples that set up the argument) are true, the conclusion will automatically follow. Let me illustrate through the following example:

> Premise 1:   if $A = B$
> Premise 2:   and $B = C$
> Conclusion: then $A = C$

Since A and B are equal, and B and C are equal, you simply exchange B for C to derive your answer. Anybody reasonable acquainted with Math 101 will see that this is true. Even an educated guess will assist the leader more often than not in making sound decisions. However, if the given information (the premises) is incorrect or misleading, setting up an equation for leadership and following it blindly, because "science says it is supposed to work," predestines one for failure. Before accepting the science, the leader must make an effort to determine the validity of the premises and weed out any information that is insufficient or irrelevant. When setting up examples in logic argumentation for the purpose of leadership, *even if* the premises are true the conclusion may NOT automatically follow. When dealing with people, sometimes common sense trumps scientific evidence:

True

if A = B
and B = C
then A = C

False

if **A**dam loves **B**ridgette
and **B**ridgette loves **C**hristopher
then **A**dam loves **C**hristopher

Although it could be true that Adam loves Christopher, it is likely false. When human emotions are involved, all logic is not true and all truth is not logic. How the leader feels about you, and how you feel about a particular issue, often determines whether or not you will cooperate and follow the leader regardless of whether or not the problem can be stated from a position of science. Thus passion often overrules logic and action must be guided by appropriate recognition of feelings. For example, if the leader treats an employee poorly, perhaps by making a derogatory remark behind the employee's back, and later apologizes, unless he is sincere in his apology, the damage cannot be repaired even if we agree in principle that an apology neutralizes an insult.

With few exceptions most conflicts are issues of passion. Even wars and world events are often issues of passion and not necessity. A team leader can therefore be passionate about an issue such as the necessity to wear a safety vest at work. But the employees can be equally passionate about not wanting to wear a safety vest. If no injuries have happened to those who do not wear the vest, and no injuries have happened to those who wear the vest, then who is correct? Does the safety vest really help prevent injuries, or do we merely think that it makes sense that it should so therefore it is mandatory to wear it? I am not arguing against safety vests or any other safety related issue, but merely demonstrating a point with respect to logic and truth. These sorts of issues can easily become a matter of who is right rather than what is right. Understanding the emotional part of human nature, no matter how illogical, may be the most important part related to success in leadership. It is important to remember that people are people first before they are workers, employees, or team members. People have emotions, and when their emotions are upset they are not likely to respond to anything the leader says. Thus before you can repair a problem you must repair the damaged emotions.

How do you guard against following logic blindly without considering whether or not it is really "truth"? You take an educated guess. If Adam loves Bridgette, and Bridgette loves Christopher, does it really make sense to say that Adam loves Christopher? When I learned how to solve equations and other mathematical problems in school, I also learned another important lesson that has saved me many times from taking the wrong fork in the road. My teacher said, "Before you do the math (the science), step back and ask what would make sense. When you have done the calculations and before insisting on the conclusion, step back and ask if it makes sense."

As a pilot and flight instructor I have applied this advice in aviation when calculating course and heading. Pilots of small aircraft use a type of plastic ruler called a plotter for this purpose, taking magnetic variation and, later, wind speed and direction into account to establish the heading. However, if you are not observant you might read the reciprocal of your course on the plotter. To avoid this mistake, I made a habit of taking an educated guess before making the actual calculations. For example, if I were going in the general direction of west, I might have guessed that the course would be somewhere in the neighborhood of 285 degrees. When I did the calculations, if it turned out to be 72 degrees, I would know that I had made a mistake and used the reciprocal because the answer was too far removed from my educated guess. If, on the other hand, my calculations gave me a number of 252 degrees, I would know that it was probably correct because, even though it differed from my educated guess by some 30 degrees, it was still in the same general direction. If you are faced with a math problem, say 7 X 8, and you plug it into the calculator and get an answer of 5.6, it should send a warning signal. If you had taken an educated guess first, you would have known that the answer calls for a much larger number.

Here is another example of why one must understand the difference between logic and truth: The FAA (Federal Aviation Administration) requires that flight instructors renew their instructor license every other year. To renew, you have two options.

You can take a refresher course and a written exam, or you can demonstrate that you have recommended at least ten students for their pilot's license exam, and that 80 percent of them passed the test. In my first two years as a flight instructor, I recommended eight students for their pilot's license tests and all of them passed; in other words, 100 percent passed. When time came to renew my instructor license, I went to the FAA office and asked the following question: "The requirement is ten students with 80 percent passing. I have signed off eight students with 100 percent passing. If you sign off ten students and eight of them pass, it is essentially the same as if you sign off eight students and eight pass. The end result in both cases is eight students passing the exam. Can I get my license renewed without taking the flight instructor refresher course?"

The FAA official scratched his head and said that he had never heard this argument before. Then he searched in the big book of regulations for an answer. When he found none, he said, "I am going to let common sense prevail and renew your license." The truth was that I had not signed off the required ten students; the logic was that I had achieved the requirement that eight students must pass the test. Truth and logic were in conflict. When truth and logic conflict, rely on common sense. Even when a good plan has been carefully crafted and defined and leads to its logical conclusion, a leader who fails to cater to human emotions will likely alienate the team. As has been demonstrated, logic and truth are not the same. All logic is not true, and all truth is not logic.

What should be learned is that the human relationships that exist at the workplace deal heavily in emotions such as love, joy, fear, anger, and frustration. These emotions determine attitudes. You can therefore not approach human emotions like you do a mathematical equation. Still, we often attempt to do just this. We claim that if people only worked together a little better, we would have a more productive environment. But if the particular people in question do not like each other, for whatever reason, they will not work well together no matter how much you wish it were so, and no matter how much "science" and statistics demonstrate that people who work well together are more productive.

As another example, we can try to convince the workforce that they should enjoy change, because change takes us away from the same mundane grind every day. However, although this might be a logical thing to say, as we have seen, it is not logical in the sense of human emotion. Most people resist change unless the change originated with them. This does not mean that the rules of logic are completely wasted when dealing with people, but it does mean that for the rules to prove useful you must understand the concepts behind logic argumentation, which state that to get people to agree with the conclusion, they we must first agree with the premises. But even then, as seen in the "If A = B" example, there will be times when logic will fall flat on its face.

What factors should you be watchful of when applying scientific or rational thinking to your leadership style? A good place to start when considering how to answer this question is by defining what you are trying to achieve in concrete terms, because it decreases the risk that you will act on impulse when implementing a new procedure. It will also help you detect incorrect information that masquerades as fact and may lead you down a faulty path. Finding one possible solution to your problem does not automatically exclude other possibilities. And do not forget to factor in uncertainty. Finally, remember that temporarily winning a heart through a clever slogan or a gung-ho speech is easy, but a broken spirit is difficult to heal.

Asking the pertinent questions is thus a prerequisite for gaining insight into the science of leadership. Those who fail to ask questions cannot lead others, because even if they know where they want to go they will not know how to get there, what happens if they take the wrong fork in the road, or how to correct a problem. Followers often ask more questions than leaders. Why? Because many leaders feel their job is to command rather than lead. Unfortunately for the leaders, this makes for a tough uphill battle. "I have taken all knowledge to be my province," said English statesman and philosopher Sir Francis Bacon (1561-1626 CE).[2] Never say "no thanks" to information. Accept what is handed to you, and decide later which parts you will take to heart and which parts you will discard.

Let's move forward and talk about why the scientific method is such a valuable asset to science, and the extent to which we can use it in the science of leadership.

THE SCIENTIFIC METHOD

A fact is a close agreement between competent people with respect to a series of observations of the same phenomenon. The catch is that the observers cannot be anybody; they must be competent. After you have defined competence, your first question might be how competence is established. Next you need a series of observations. Observing something once does not help you establish a fact. You must also consider the frame of reference, defined as a vantage point with respect to the position and motion of an object. Depending on where you stand, your frame of reference may differ from somebody else's. You may not see what somebody else sees and may therefore make false assumptions. In a scientific sense this idea can be related to *parallax*, which we will talk more about a little later.

To even begin to solve a problem, you must be curious enough to want to experiment with it. The issue must be on your mind enough that you feel a legitimate need to do something about it. How do you determine if your need is legitimate? It is easy to fall prey to our own capacity to fool ourselves. Some leaders are so certain that an issue needs to be addressed or changed that they decide on a solution before running it through the required steps of scientific analysis. Physical scientists, by contrast, approach problems from an unbiased standpoint; they abstain from deciding beforehand what science is to reveal. In fact:

> [T]he true mark of science (as opposed to its many masquerades) is an attempt to refute one's hypothesis, to be self-critical, to examine one's assumptions, and to point out ways to further test one's theory . . . Science makes probabilistic claims; it is not usually about proving that something is always the case, or never the case. Almost all science is about showing a greater probability that something is usually the case . . . The preponderance of the evidence represents scientific knowledge.[3]

To fully appreciate the laws of science and leadership, you must understand the rules. If you skip a step or work in reverse, you will create a chain reaction of strategic mistakes that may take years to fix, or that cannot be fixed. If you implement plans and procedures without truly understanding the underlying reasons, you will lose the trust of your team, be predestined for failure, and later try to save face when your team has thrashed you. The scientific method is a good place to start because it sort of covers your bases. How does it work? First recognize that you have a problem. If you don't know that you have a problem, it will be difficult to solve it. Next make an educated guess. The guess must be reasonably related to the problem. Then predict the consequences. This is called forming a *hypothesis*. When you have made an educated guess, forming the hypothesis is easier. Then test the hypothesis to determine if your educated guess has merit and your prediction is valid. Finally formulate a rule as simple and straight forward as possible intended to correct the problem.

Although scientific principles are great teachers, when searching for the science (the discovery of evidence and relationships) all hypotheses (the predictions of the consequences) must be testable. In other words, for the predictions to be valid there must be a way of proving them wrong. For example, if you work in the service industry, you might be inclined to implement a rule that requires your employees to address the customers by name. Your prediction is that this will foster a friendly atmosphere that benefits your business interests. Your next step is to perform an experiment to test the hypothesis. You give each customer a questionnaire asking whether they are more or less likely to do business with you as a result of being addressed by name. You now have your employees test the rule, record the findings over a period of time, and compare the results to those you acquired prior to the new rule taking effect.

You may now have constructed a test that will help you determine if the implementation of the new rule will help or hinder your business. The test is valid because the questionnaire and the employee testing of the rule over time have provided a way of proving your predictions wrong. Your predictions do not *have* to be proven wrong, but *there must be a way* of proving them wrong for the test to be valid in a scientific sense. For example, if you saw no change or if you saw a decline in business when the rule of addressing the customer by name was brought into effect, you would scrap the rule. By contrast, if the questionnaire did not provide the customer with a way of voicing a negative opinion, and if you neglected to run a comparison of results, you would not have provided the test subjects with a way of proving the hypothesis wrong. You would therefore not have gained any insight into the validity of the new procedure, at least not in a scientific sense.

Consider this: A common irritant when phoning a company for help is that you have to listen to a recording stating that "for quality assurance, this call may be monitored." Then you have to press one for English or two for Spanish. Then you will get a lengthy menu from which to choose a suitable action. Since many callers will be more than a little annoyed by now, the company's goal of customer satisfaction through monitoring the phone calls is defeated by the recording that says so and by the lengthy recorded menus. If you are an employee forced to address the customer by name or say, "Thanks for choosing (enter your company name here)," and are rated on how well you use this script, if the script fails to make the customer feel greater satisfaction, it defeats the purpose. In fact, reading a script could have the effect of making the customer believe that you are incapable of or uninterested in showing genuine concern for his or her problems. You can also misuse the scientific method by leaving out steps, reversing the chain, or failing to ask the proper questions. For example, if you *assume* that people will turn to your business when they are addressed by name (perhaps because you like to be addressed by name), but you never actually run the experiments or ask why, you may or may not be correct in your assumption, but either way, you have not gained any true insight that you can use to your benefit later.

The ability to properly discern scientific relationships is often the result of an enormous amount of knowledge. Intellectual growth comes from the encouragement of open-minded debate, not from the memorization of and ability to restate the principles. For example, if you desire to change employee attitudes toward their jobs, it is insufficient to acknowledge that the goals of the company must coincide with the goals of the employees. You must go a step further and finish the thought by defining exactly what those goals are. You might also want to run your vision through some logic argumentation to determine if the employees and the company in fact agree on the premises. As demonstrated in the equation involving Adam, Bridgette, and Christopher, a system that is so rigid that it makes no allowances for human emotion tends to make leadership science meaningless.

Although the scientific method is a good place to start, it is not the only place. You can also make an effort to understand what those opposed to an idea are really saying. When analyzing a problem, learn to distinguish between what you see and what you wish to see. Be ready to accept your findings even if they are not what you wish them to be. When you refrain from shielding yourself from those opposing your ideas and instead strive to understand them in the proper context, you will set yourself up for intellectual growth. You don't have to do everything that your opposition is asking of you, but you do have to understand it. A principle may be a starting point as long as it is open to critique. When employees are allowed to critique widely, we eliminate much subjectivity and decrease the risk of using the limited scope of a single leader's mind as a standard.

ONE SIZE DOES NOT FIT ALL

How does the team fit into the science of leadership? A problem with many leadership slogans is that they tell us what the goal is without giving specific examples of what needs to be done. For example, the goal is to get the employees to "work as a team focused on excellence and innovation in business." But how exactly do you get people to work as a team toward this goal? How do you define team? What does it mean to be a team player? What if somebody is a loner? Does this mean that he or she cannot be a productive part of a team? How do you help the team attain and maintain focus? Telling the employees that they must focus will most certainly not be enough. How do you define excellence? Give some specific examples. What does innovation mean? These words may seem self-explanatory, but are they really? If you fail to define, you will also fail to communicate clearly. When you fail to communicate, it will be difficult to get others to agree. And when you cannot reach agreement, your mission will likely fail. Remember that to get others to agree with the conclusion you must first get them to agree with the premises.

It is also important to understand that you cannot be all to everybody. It's been said that it is better to stand for something than to stand for everything. When communicating with your employees, ask yourself whether you are honest and avoid communicating values as if they were facts. My guess is that you will say about yourself that you are honest, but consider also how others perceive you. If you are in the habit of looking at the floor whenever you pass somebody in the hallway, the employees may falsely translate your behavior as dishonesty. There is a fitting parable:

> A dog was chasing a rabbit, but when he caught the rabbit he didn't know what to do with his prey. First he bit the rabbit, and then he licked the rabbit and wagged his tail. The rabbit said, "What is the meaning with all this? If you don't want to harm me, then why do you bite me? And if you do want to harm me, then why do you lick me and wag your tail?" Conclusion? It is better with an honest foe than an inconsistent friend. At least you know what you've got.

The team is not for everybody. As politically wrong as it sounds, to maintain pride the team must discriminate; it must include some people and exclude others. If you were a top-rated football player, would you really be happy playing on a team where some of the members were allowed to skip tryouts and practice and play anyway, no matter how lousy they were? Likewise, a top-rated team in the workplace is not a *one-size-fits-all* concept. This is the same idea that gives the Marines the right to call themselves "the few, the proud." Pride comes from knowing that you are unique, stronger, and better than the competition. Winning matters. Teamwork is not about creating a win-win situation. Rather, the team is zero-sum: We win, you lose. It matters less whose team you are on as long as you are on the winning team. (We admire Napoleon Bonaparte, not because he had great character, but because he knew how to win. As a mental exercise, even though it might be a disgusting one, consider how we might feel about Adolf Hitler, had Germany emerged victorious in World War II.) If your company is failing, would you feel as proud to work there?

And yes, size matters, too. If the team needs nine members to function and you are number ten, you are the one they don't need. If the team needs ten members to function and you are number ten, you are the piece that makes the puzzle whole. Exactly how many members does the team need? Or is this even an issue? Perhaps it is as simple as saying that bigger is better? Think about it: If everybody works for the same company and toward the same goal, it would seem natural that a big team would have a greater driving force. This hypothetical example does not take cost into consideration. In other words, you don't need to be concerned with whether or not a big team is cost effective at the moment. So if payroll is not an issue, is bigger still better? If money is not an issue, bigger may sound better. But consider this: When groups are too large, smaller groups tend to form within the larger groups, and as a result everyone on the team will not care about everyone else. You will thus be stuck with the "us vs. them" mentality, which naturally goes against the grain of team building. For empirical evidence, particularly if you work for a large company, you might want to take a peek into the break room on any given day and observe how certain employees tend to group together and form natural "teams."

Each team member must also be needed and know that the team cannot function without him or her. A team that is too large will have many members with overlapping skills and, therefore, some members will be expendable. As a result each member's importance is reduced. Would it be true to say that the company where you work, which has a branch in almost every state of the Union, is a single team? Or would it be truer to say that the branch in Denver is one team and the branch in New York is another team? If you visit the branch in Denver, would you say that the workers in the five different departments within this branch are on the same team? Or is it truer to say that they are on different teams? If your company hires contract workers as part of the workforce, are they on the same team as the regulars or on a different team? If you limit the size of the team, should you treat the members of your particular team the same as the members of another team within your company? Why, or why not? Now let's say that you are in charge of several smaller departments. How would you go about increasing cooperation and teamwork between different departments? What are some of the barriers you might run into regarding support from other teams within your company? When you attempt to break barriers, is there a risk that you are actually creating more barriers?

At one place of employment there were almost eight hundred workers in a particular building. For many years these workers were split into smaller teams. That is until management came up with the not so brilliant idea that all workers should be grouped together into one large team; throw all names in a hat, so to speak. Why? For cross-utilization and to break barriers, they said. Not wanting to split from their particular team and buddies, the work group protested heavily. But management told them that since there is no "I" in team, it should not matter where they work or with whom. When this concept went into effect, many of the employees stopped caring about the customer. Why? Because grouping everybody together killed their motivation; they no longer felt that they had ownership of their particular department or work area; they were unable to identify with the team. But what about the customer, you may ask? After all, it is not the customer's fault that management killed the workers' motivation and acted so poorly and with so little forethought. Well, yes. However, the team does not work for the customer. Each team member works for the other members on the team. The reason why is because it is the team and not the customer who gives the members their identity. Good customer service is a byproduct of a well-run team. If you want good customer service you must first fix the team.

With the foregoing in mind, let's look at the team from a scientific perspective and use a concept from physics to illustrate a principle.

WHO STOLE "I" FROM TEAM?

Molecules are the building blocks of all that exists. They are the smallest units of any substance, and are composed of clusters of atoms with particular properties. The way the atoms combine determines the types and properties of the molecules. The stronger the bonds between atoms are, the stronger the molecule. Diamonds, for example, are very hard because the carbon atoms of the diamond are connected by strong chemical bonds. But a molecule can also be as simple as a combination of two like atoms, as is the case with oxygen. Some of the simplest molecules, like oxygen and water, also have the greatest life-sustaining properties. Just as molecules vary in strength and contain a combination of properties, a functional team must be varied and strong and contain a combination of qualities including those that are complex and those that are simple. English physicist Sir Isaac Newton (1642-1727 CE) used a prism to discover that he could split light into the colors of the rainbow, and how all wavelengths of light when mixed formed into a white beam. This observation is analogous to the parts that make up a unit, or what we call the whole. Although each part has different qualities, the particles can blend into a single unit. With this in mind I would like to ask, who stole "I" from team?

"There is no I in team," is one of the most overused and abused team sayings. No matter who you are or where you work, you will no doubt remember some sport coach, supervisor, or motivational speaker telling you just this. No doubt will you remember somebody's calendar posted on somebody's office wall displaying this particular slogan. And, yes, it is easy to agree without giving it further thought. After all, who can argue that by definition a team must comprise more than one person? Who can argue that it is the team's cohesiveness and ability to work as one that makes it strong, that strength is in numbers, that nobody won a war with a one-man army, and that if you place your own comfort and well-being ahead of the team, you will likely get ousted from the team? But without defining, we have, in fact, gained no more insight than we would have by saying that it is raining, which in and of itself is neither good nor bad. If you are a farmer battling months of drought, you will no doubt be delighted at the rainfall. If you are going on a picnic for your child's tenth birthday, you will more likely be of the opinion that somebody literally "rained on your parade."

The "no I in team" concept refers not to the actual spelling of the word *team*, of course, as this idea would have no relation to leadership or team play whatsoever. However, the assumption is that since there is no "I" in the word *team* (literally), there should be no "I" in the actual teamwork concept either. Is this a good assumption? Is it logic? I don't think so. Why not? Because A does not logically lead to B for the simple reason that grammar and teamwork are not even remotely related. In fact, if you went to a different country, you may well find an "I" in the word for *team* in that country's language. In the pinyin Romanization of Chinese Mandarin, for example, the word for team is *dui*. (Look, there is an "I" in it!) Does this mean that a principle that is true for us Americans is untrue in China? Of course not! The saying is a play on words, nothing more, and the saying cannot automatically be transformed into any particular truths about teamwork. As emphasized in the excellent book, *First, Break All the Rules*, by Marcus Buckingham and Curt Coffman, "The point here seems to be that teams are built on collaboration and mutual support. The whole is apparently more important than its individual parts." However, a productive team is "one where each person knows which role he plays best and where he is cast in that role most of the time."[4]

Why should we care about "no I in team" if we don't also have some way of associating ourselves with the deeper meaning of teamwork? The saying is in principle as meaningful (or meaningless) as describing the American flag as thirteen stripes for the original states and fifty stars for the current states. Who cares about the stars and the stripes, if we don't also have some way of associating ourselves with the meaning of our flag?

People *die* for our flag! Why?

People die for our flag because it is a symbol of our identity; it's who we are. Take a look at your company's widget. You have seen it a hundred times. If I asked you to describe it, and all you did was state the facts; its colors and shapes, then you are missing the boat. A flag, an emblem, and a widget serve to unite a people. You raise the flag and pledge allegiance to it because you identify with it. How you perform has a lot to do with your identity; in other words, how you feel about yourself. Go to the ski-hill, the beach, or the gym and observe how people dress and act. Some people feel "cool" dressing up, others feel cool dressing casual; some people like bright colors, others like earth tones. But we all want to feel cool (or hot, for that matter). If you could dress any way you wanted, what would you wear? If you could drive any car you wanted, what would you drive? Why? When we feel cool about ourselves, we are "in the zone," we are in tune with ourselves. We have an identity. We know who we are. This is the essence of teamwork.

Once you start dissecting the saying, you will begin to see that the idea is more complex than what first meets our ears; that it has implications that extend far beyond the saying itself. The team must function as a unit; this is part of the meaning of "no I in team." A unit has all its parts so interrelated that it looks like one. In physics, atoms are the building blocks of molecules and form a substance with specific bonds and qualities, such as strength (a diamond) or life (water). The company where you work may be a unit outwardly. You know it because of the company colors and widgets on the equipment and worker uniforms. You know it because of the slogans. Yet a functional team must be both varied and strong. To function as a unit, all parts must be so interrelated that it looks like one. But its strength—and this is important—lies not in the similarities of the many parts that make it up, but in the *differences*. Take a jigsaw puzzle. When completed, it forms a perfect picture, yet no two parts look the same. Each team member holds an intricate piece of the puzzle. If you were building a brick wall, you would stagger the bricks for strength. Likewise, a diamond is strong because of the complexity of the bonds between the atoms. How should a team be constructed for strength, then?

If the relationship between the different parts is not honed, the unit will fail. If the unit fails, each individual part (team member) will also fail. This is what we mean when we say "one for all—all for one." Simultaneously, we must understand why it is important who gets the credit. Thus your job as a team leader is not to promote a team that is uniform, but to build a team with complementary qualities. Throughout the rest of your study keep these simple concepts in mind, and when asked what comes first, the team or the individual, remember that although molecules are the building blocks of all that exists, atoms are the building blocks of molecules just as individuals are the building blocks of teams.

Let's look at the "I-chain" inherent to a successfully run team. (With some ingenuity, you might think of plenty more parts to include in this chain.) If you break the chain, you break the strength of the team:

1. **I**dentity
2. **I**ndividualism
3. **S**ize
4. **I**mportance
5. **I**nclusion-Exclusion
6. Pride
7. **I**ntelligence
8. **I**ntegrity

A successful team contains **identity**, or the unique need of the individual to be part of the team. Identity is established through team colors, songs, uniforms, slogans, and widgets. **Individualism** is the ability of each member to experience the value he or she brings to the team. Note that although individualism should be encouraged rather than dampened, it must still be managed. There must be certain guidelines, for example, in dress code and safety; there must be some kind of protocol to follow for accomplishing the job in accordance with the company's image. Too much freedom or individualism without staying within the values of the organization results in a loss of identity rather than in a stronger team. It could also jeopardize safety and customer service. Performing according to a set procedure also allows us to transfer what we learn to our peers. If everybody develops their own way of doing things, the "system" becomes un-teachable; we are ignoring the primary thing that makes us human: our ability to transfer knowledge and findings to others without reinventing the wheel. Transferring knowledge through tested and managed procedures helps us accelerate learning and make improvements.

Size is directly related to how well the team can function as a unit. A team that is too large will prevent the members from feeling ownership, and a team that is too small will prevent the members from functioning efficiently. And, of course, it matters who gets the credit, because receiving proper credit for a job well done increases motivation and pride. Thus, **importance** becomes part of the "I-chain." Importance also leads to **inclusion-exclusion**, which helps maintain **pride**. The team must discriminate by including those individuals who contribute to the strength of the team while excluding freeloaders. Although a great many of us would die for our flag, at what point would we turn around and say that we have sacrificed enough? Although the ideal is something to live, fight, and even die for, our pride needs constant reinforcement to remain a motivating force. And from a competitive standpoint, it doesn't make sense to include the competition in our team strategies. The team must therefore be exclusive of the competition and of those members whose actions serve to sabotage the cohesiveness of the team. The principle of inclusion-exclusion allows the team members to identify with the team, yet discriminate by understanding the boundaries of the team. A word of caution: Everybody does not have the same ability to work fast or be organized. This is a result of people's differences in age, genetic makeup, etc., and does not automatically mean that those who fall short of your expectations are freeloaders. You must keep individual circumstances and characteristics in mind before criticizing other team members. Ask instead if a person's work really represents his or her best efforts.

Can you use science or statistical data to determine how much work is appropriate for an employee? Can you use scientific evidence to weed out the slackers? Let's say that at the company where you work, some people consistently unload eight freight trucks per day, while others unload only six. If you look at the statistics alone, you might draw the conclusion that those who unload more trucks are the better workers. However, you must also consider that those who unload more trucks have to unload only ten pallets per truck, and not twenty pallets that the supposedly slower workers unload. Now, who are the better workers? Is the person who shoots the most baskets necessarily the best player? Or is he simply selfish by refusing to pass the ball to a team member? By removing the people who unload fewer trucks from your workforce, you might actually be removing the keystone of support for your team, and not the slow or lazy workers as you might have thought when you first reviewed the statistics.

Intelligence prevents the leader from misjudging situations that place the team in danger or ridicule. And **integrity** contributes to the cohesiveness of the team. The leader does not own the team physically, mentally, or emotionally. Once everybody understands this, the leader can with good conscience lead his team toward the goal. Think about this: If you need the support of your customers or other "outside people," how would you go about balancing integrity between the customers and your team? At what point do you need to take sides, and whose side should you take? Why? Who should be included and who should be excluded when conflicts arise? How do you create a winning team? You find a leader who uses intelligence and common sense. The leader establishes himself or herself as credible through integrity, or truthfulness and honesty. So, you see, it is easy to babble about "no I in team" and "Together Everybody Achieves More." It is easier to be a yeah-sayer than to think the thought to conclusion.

Now that we know why the individual is important to the team, let's look at how the qualities of the individual can strengthen the team if properly understood and utilized, and sabotage the team if not.

TEAM VERSUS INDIVIDUAL EXCELLENCE

Marcus Buckingham and Curt Coffman, authors of the highly recommended book, *First, Break All the Rules*, and leaders of The Gallup Organization's effort to identify great workplaces, offer the following insights into team optimization and the value of the individual:

> In the early nineties, one of the leading hospitality companies began experimenting with self-managed work teams as a replacement for the traditional manager role . . . To encourage individual growth, each employee would be able to increase his pay only by learning how to play each of the other roles on the team . . . It was an inspired plan, with only one flaw: It did not work . . . The best housekeepers did not want to become front-desk clerks. They liked housekeeping. Front-desk clerks did not like table serving, and table servers did not appreciate the mess the front-desk clerks were making of their precious restaurant. Each employee came to feel as though he were in the wrong role. He no longer knew exactly what was expected of him. He no longer felt competent, and with the focus on team rather than individual

excellence, he no longer felt important.[5]

The study further says: "One team member might occasionally have to step out of his role to support another, but this kind of pinch-hitting should be a rarity on great teams, not their very essence. Whereas conventional wisdom views individual specialization as the antithesis of teamwork, great managers see it as the founding principle."[6]

A word of caution for those who want to optimize teamwork by cross-utilizing employees: To optimize means to achieve the best possible outcome every time. Team optimization is therefore a concept that allows us to reach the BEST (not just a good) outcome in ANY circumstance (not just on occasion). Cross-utilization does not produce an optimized team. A team that is supposedly optimized through cross-utilization will likely be no team at all. What is supposed to bring the employees together will instead have the opposite effect of sabotaging the team concept. Many employees will no longer know exactly what is expected of them. Many will no longer feel competent, and with the focus on (team) optimization rather than individual excellence, many employees will no longer feel validated or important. Loss of pride will follow, with a subsequent loss in customer service. As a leader in a world class company, is this really what you want?

The reason why people excel is because they have had the opportunity to perfect their skills in one specific area. When selecting your team, it is better to look for varied abilities between the people than for varied abilities within the same person. When you have hired your people to perform a specific job and suddenly ask them to do another job or take on additional duties not in their job description, the reason why you run into difficulties may be related to the fact that the people you hired are specialists in their specific areas, and asking them to do other jobs actually means that you are trying to capitalize on their weaknesses and not on their strengths.

The Gallup Organization has also put together a list of questions intended to measure the strength of a workplace and the core elements needed to attract, focus, and keep the most talented employees. This list is a result of the findings from interviews conducted with hundreds of companies, managers, and employees.[7] As an employee evaluating the strength of your workplace, you should strive for as many "yes" answers as possible. Then, and in order to think the thought to conclusion, give an example that supports your answer.

1. Do I know what is expected of me at work?

2. Do I have the materials and equipment I need to do my work right?

3. At work, do I have the opportunity to do what I do best every day?

4. In the last seven days, have I received recognition or praise for doing good work?

5. Does my supervisor, or someone at work, seem to care about me as a person?

6. Is there someone at work who encourages my development?

7. At work, do my opinions seem to count?

8. Does the mission/purpose of my company make me feel my job is important?

9. Are my co-workers committed to doing quality work?

10. Do I have a best friend at work?

11. In the last six months, has someone at work talked to me about my progress?

12. This last year, have I had opportunities at work to learn and grow?

Let's take a moment and explore question 10: Do I have a best friend at work? Having a best friend at work makes you look forward to coming to work. However, one may wonder what a best friend has got to do with teamwork, or how the team leader is supposed to have control over this issue? Here is the problem: If an employee has a best friend at work, but the team leader prevents the employee from working together with his or her friend whenever possible, the many good qualities that go along with friendship, such as a feeling of joy and looking forward to coming to work, are sabotaged. This is one of the core concepts of a cohesive team: The team members must WANT to form a team; a team is not just ANY group of people. People who like each other and want to work together should therefore be placed together.

Efficient teamwork is about developing the qualities you find in each team member, and not trying to make each member what he or she is not. When the employees at one particular corporation desired a change in work habits and delivered a petition to the manager, he rebutted by explaining that a petition "is not our way." But who is the judge? Who determines whose "way" it is when tens of thousands of men and women are employed at this corporation? Who is to say what is safer, more fun, or provides better opportunities? Why is it not only difficult but a bad idea to be the judge for others by defining their objectives for them? It might be wise now to consider the nearly two thousand years old insights of Petronius Arbiter (c. 27-66 CE), a Roman courtier:

> We trained hard . . . but it seemed that every time we were beginning to form up into teams, we would be reorganized. I was to learn later in life that we tend to meet any new situation by reorganizing; and a wonderful method it can be for creating the illusion of progress while producing confusion, inefficiency, and demoralization.[8]

To reemphasize, you cannot throw together any number of employees and call it a team. The reason why a large team has a greater potential to be a motivation killer than a small team, is because each member on a large team tends to become only a number. In other words, individual identity is lost. Another problem with a large team is that each member will also be shielded from pain and the effects of wrongdoing. Specific responsibilities cannot be delegated because we assume that "it is everybody's responsibility," and everybody's responsibility becomes nobody's responsibility. So what exactly is the proper size of the team? This is a difficult question to answer, which is yet a reason why science, which deals with precise numbers and concepts, often cannot be used successfully when dealing with people. However, a good guideline when contemplating team size is to start by defining the tasks the team needs to accomplish and the number of members needed for each task. Then strive to make the team small enough to make no member expendable, and specific enough to bring about feelings of ownership and pride.

Now that you have pondered the previous material, if you still prefer to Lead with Science, the next section will deal with some scientific terms that might give you a good start.[9] As you consider each term and how it might relate to team leadership, make sure you also define each term precisely to detect potential pitfalls.

WAYS TO LEAD WITH SCIENCE

Science is about discovering evidence and relationships for observable phenomena, and establishing theories that organize and make sense of those phenomena. **Technology** is about the tools, techniques, and procedures we use for implementing the scientific findings. If we know the principles but don't have the capacity to utilize them, we are not very successful as leaders. The opposite is also true. If we apply the technology, the methods and techniques, but don't understand the underlying principles, we may end up using the wrong tools and will be unable to perform the job satisfactorily. The **scientific method** is a good place to start, because it organizes our thoughts in the proper sequence and decreases the risk of making mistakes. There are a number of steps that must be followed: Recognize that there is a problem, make an educated guess and predict the consequences (form a hypothesis), perform experiments to test the predictions, and formulate the simplest general rule that organizes the hypothesis and experimental outcome into a theory.

The scientific method thus helps us establish a procedure for finding the facts about a particular issue. What is a fact? A **fact** is a close agreement between competent observers of a series of observations of the same phenomenon. As previously noted, the observers must be *competent*. Depending on their background and competence, the opinions or findings of one person might carry greater weight than the opinions and findings of another. When related to team leadership, the employee is probably the person with the greatest competence when it comes to determining whether or not he or she should embrace a particular change. This is not the same as saying that the employee is qualified to determine, for example, whether or not cutbacks in personnel are necessary to make the company profitable; only that the employee is the authority on whether or not he will embrace or resist cutbacks in personnel. If the leadership tells an employee that he should go to the fish market in Seattle to learn about positive attitudes at work because it is so much fun, but the employee's idea of fun differs from management's, who is the better judge? Who is the more competent "observer"? Who has the facts? The employee is the more competent observer, because he or she alone determines what fun means to him or her in particular.

A **hypothesis**, on the other hand, is an educated guess; a reasonable explanation of an observation of experimental results that is not fully accepted as factual, but that can be used to guide us toward a fact. Before we can establish a new law in science, or a new policy in the workplace, we must form a hypothesis. The problem is that we often tend to jump to conclusions based on the hypothesis without doing sufficient experimentation. Or, worse, we might skip the hypothesis altogether and proceed with a change without even considering, or guessing, how the workforce will react. **Elasticity**, for example, is the ability to change shape when a force is applied and return to the original shape when the force is removed. In teamwork elasticity can be related to flexibility. How many times have you heard that you must be flexible and bend with the forces if you want to realize success? The question of importance is how far a material can be stretched without permanent distortion, or how far a team can be stretched or asked to change before losing motivation and refusing to spring back to its optimum shape.

Hooke's Law states that the extension of an elastic object is directly proportional to the stretching force applied. The **elastic limit** is the distance beyond which permanent distortion occurs. In leadership it is important to have a good sense of the location of this limit or breaking point. Simultaneously keep in mind that an inelastic object, or a team that resists change, tends to be more fragile and break more easily than an elastic object and must therefore be treated more delicately if you want to avoid sabotaging the positive qualities of the team. **Pressure**, by contrast, is the ratio of force to the area over which that force is distributed. When you apply a large force to a small area you will exert a lot of pressure, and vice versa. You must therefore have a fine sense of how much pressure your team can handle before it stops functioning properly. You must similarly decide how to distribute that pressure so that it doesn't fall on just a few members of the team. You can think of pressure in terms of workload. How many employees do you need to hire to reach maximum efficiency at minimum cost? How do you handle those who are ambitious versus those who are lazy? Do you put more pressure on the ambitious employees and less on the lazy, or vice versa? Why?

Furthermore, to answer the question of how far a team can be stretched or asked to change before losing motivation and refusing to spring back to its optimum shape, we must understand something about teams, their composition, and how the individual parts interact with one another. In physics, **molecules** are tiny parts that make up living as well as non-living things. The more complex the molecular pattern the stronger the object. A team can be viewed as a complex organism where total strength rests in the differences and not similarities between individuals. However, exactly how a team should look to achieve its goal, or what type of "molecule" will be most beneficial, must also be determined. Although complex makes strong, some of the simplest molecules like water and oxygen are also the most life sustaining. So just how complex should your team be? How inclusive should it be of new team members? Remember that when bringing new members in, the "atoms" that build the molecules must rearrange, giving you a **chemical reaction** that could manifest as a violent explosion.

A **change of state** in the molecular structure can also occur when heat is absorbed, which causes the molecules to vibrate more and more violently. When enough heat is absorbed, the attractive forces between the molecules will no longer hold them together. Bonds will break. Think about how this applies to teamwork. When the bonds between individuals break due to too much "steam" within the team, the group will become unstable and unable to function as a unit. Steam has even more potential energy than boiling water, because the molecules are relatively free to move about and even a slight disturbance will set them off. By contrast, if too little heat is applied, all energy is withdrawn and the group will lose motivation and become lethargic. One way to use this concept when Leading with Science is to relate it to motivation. How do you find the correct balance between the gung-ho leader (or team) and the pacifist who doesn't seem to care much one way or the other?

To keep a constant flow of energy you must consistently apply pressure, but not so much that it breaks the bonds between team members and destroys unity. The phenomenon of melting under pressure and freezing again when the pressure is reduced is called **regelation**, and can be applied to the employee's relation to supervision and management. The employee may be more likely to comply with requests when there is pressure to do so. But when the pressure is removed or the supervisor is not looking, the employee will return to the old behavior.

As discussed previously, a fully functioning team must have members with complementary qualities. **Complementary** means "mutually exclusive." Think of this as the yin-yang symbol. Only the union of yin-yang forms a whole. With respect to leadership, this concept can be likened to how one part, branch, or department of a company cannot function without another. The company cannot function without the customers; management cannot function without the workers, and vice versa. The customer is not always right, but neither is the company. The boss is not always right, but neither is the employee. Each group must complement the others to form a whole, or what we call a workable and efficient team.

With respect to determining the proper size of the team for optimum unit cohesion, we can consider **vector quantities** that have both magnitude and direction. It is not only important how big something is, but also in what direction it is moving. We might want to remember that as the size of an object increases, the object grows heavier much faster than it grows stronger. This is called **scaling**. Thus bigger doesn't necessarily translate into stronger, which is why it is crucial to understand that a team has an optimum size that allows it to function as a unit where members can bond properly and avoid wasting energy. Cohesion, of course, is an important team concept. In physics, **cohesion** is the attraction between like substances, and **adhesion** is the attraction between unlike substances. Perhaps it is adhesion rather than cohesion that should be considered when building a team. As explored earlier, a team with too many similar qualities between its members will be less strong than a team with unlike but complementary qualities.

Once you have established a proper composition for your team, the next step is to put it to work. **Energy** is defined as anything that can change the condition of matter or has the ability to do work. Conservation of energy and the **First Law of Thermodynamics** states that energy output can never exceed energy input. If many years pass where there is no inflow of energy, or no motivation, the workforce will become lethargic. By contrast, when you add energy to a system such as a team, it can convert that energy to a different form and produce work that helps the company achieve the desired results. The **Second Law of Thermodynamics** states that heat will never flow by itself from a cold object to a hot object. Heat (like the proverbial shit) flows only one way: downhill from hot to cold. This is why, when the supervisor takes "heat" from his superiors, the employees will surely take heat from the supervisor in the near future. We can also think of this as "passing the buck." Unfortunately, the buck is normally passed in a negative sense.

Natural systems further tend to proceed toward a state of greater disorder or randomness, producing a lot of waste. Disordered energy can be changed to ordered energy only at the expense of some organizational effort. **Entropy** is the measure of the amount of disorder. Whenever a physical system is allowed to distribute its energy freely, entropy generally increases, resulting in a decrease in ability of the available energy to do work. This is why we need leadership. When entropy occurs, there must be an input of energy to restore the strength of the original system. When a team is allowed to break apart, it takes more energy to restore it to its original shape than the amount of energy that was lost through entropy. This is why first impressions are important and why it is difficult to remedy a leadership faux pas. Every change you implement that is perceived by the team in negative terms will create a slight loss from the "original." Liken this to using a copy machine. The copy will never be of the same quality as the original, and each time you make a copy of each new copy, the worse it will appear. No machine can be completely efficient in converting energy to work, and all systems tend to become more and more disorganized as time goes by. If not managed, organized systems will eventually decay and descend into chaos; that is, unless the system is open and allows for proper transfer of energy.

If energy can change the condition of matter and has the ability to do work, then what is work?

Work is the force times the distance, and **power** is the work done over a particular time interval. If you can move an object over a short distance, little work is required for a given force. If you can move an object in a short time, you have a lot of power. But since energy is what enables you to do work, if you want to do a lot of work you must think of a way to conserve energy (perhaps by working smarter and not harder). No machine or device can put out more energy than is put into it. Although it can multiply force, it cannot multiply energy. How **efficient** something is can be expressed by the ratio of work done over energy used. Thus if you are very efficient, you can do a lot of work without expending a lot of energy. If you expend a lot of energy, you ought to rethink how you do the work. When there is inefficiency, much energy is wasted. Work that does not lead to results is a waste of energy. A prime example is what is popularly referred to as "busy work," delegated to employees when management doesn't like them sitting idle. Busy work does not make a company more efficient. Busy work and inefficiency in general also tends to have a negative effect on employee pride and motivation; it tends to destroy the team's momentum.

    Momentum means inertia in motion, and **inertia** means resistance to change. The faster an object moves and the heavier it is, the more difficult it is to stop its motion or reverse its direction. As discussed previously, people resist change; it's natural to resist change and not easily overcome. When you try to implement change, there *will* be inertia. Implementing change in the workplace is particularly difficult when you need to convince a large group of people of your views, particularly if these people are already opposed to your views. You must not only stop their current motion which is directing them away from your views, you must also start motion in a new direction. Change in direction means a change in momentum because a component part of the momentum equation is **velocity**, or speed and direction. An alternative to stopping the motion, or slowing it down when desiring to change the momentum, is to change the direction through the application of an outside force.

Impulse is another way to look at the change in momentum. A large change in momentum in a short time requires a large force. Thus implementing a sudden rather than gradual change will require a large force. **Forces**, whether small or large, always occur in pairs with each force acting in the opposite direction of the other. Or, according to **Newton's Third Law of Motion**, to every action there is an equal and opposite reaction. So when you exert a force in the workplace, you create an *interaction* between yourself and the person against whom you exert the force. It is thus unreasonable to exert a force against a person without also expecting to feel the effects of that force. **Friction** is a force resisting motion. Since it takes energy to overcome friction, you should evaluate beforehand how much friction the change in a procedure is likely to cause among the employees, and whether or not it will be worth the effort. Friction always acts in a direction opposing motion. Moreover, **irregularities** act as obstructions to motion. When we fail to agree on issues, we have irregularities and therefore friction. When implementing a change that your employees resist, to overcome friction you must first apply a force that is equal to the force of friction just to reach neutral ground. When this has been done, you must apply an additional force to get the employees moving in the new direction. Change can therefore be tremendously energy consuming and troublesome. If possible you want to start negotiations for change from a position of minimal friction between your views and those of the employees.

You must also be aware of a possible **chain reaction**, or a self-sustaining reaction that once started steadily provides the energy and matter necessary to continue the reaction. A chain reaction can provide a great effect through little energy. Before starting an action (a change in policy, for example), you must therefore look at the possible consequences and the probability that the action will turn into a chain reaction. Negative information can be intensified through a chain reaction, and if you are not careful have undesirable consequences that will spiral out of control. Furthermore, when different substances rub against or touch one another there is a **charge by contact**. By contrast, **charging by induction** is the redistribution of charges in and on objects caused by the electrical influence of an object nearby but not in contact. When using this idea in the workplace, you can feel the effects of another person's mood or behavior even if he or she is not directing the behavior toward you in particular. Rather, the atmosphere around this person gets "charged," either positively or negatively.

Do waves within the team make it stronger or weaker? Wave motion can tell you something about the source that is producing the wave. A **wave** is the transfer of energy from a source to a distance receiver without the transfer of actual matter between the two points. As mentioned previously, if a rock is dropped into a pond waves will travel outward in expanding circles. But if the wave experiences an obstacle such as a concrete wall, the water will run back into the pond and things will be much as they were before the initial disturbance. Although the water in the pond was disturbed it did not go anywhere or accomplish anything, and the medium returned to its original condition after the disturbance had ceased. With respect to leadership we can think of the transfer of information within an organization in terms of waves. Or we can think of waves as the transfer of energy from one employee to another. When energy is transferred between employees, the group as a whole may be motivated to perform a task.

In physics, the speed of the wave is equal to its frequency times the wavelength. A short wavelength translates into a high frequency or a more violent disturbance, and vice versa. Moreover, a single location is not limited to one vibration or wave. Also, as discussed previously, if you drop two rocks into water, the waves produced by each can overlap and form an interference pattern. Within this pattern, wave effects may be increased, decreased, or neutralized. Waves may be reinforced in some places and cancelled in others by this interference pattern. When the crest of one wave overlaps the crest of another their individual effects are summarized, called **constructive interference**. With respect to team leadership we can say that the two waves have in effect team worked to produce an overall stronger wave. However, be aware that the term constructive can be misleading. Increasing the overall effect of the wave does not necessarily mean that you achieve an overall more positive outcome. **Destructive interference**, where you calm the effect and flatten the wave, may in fact be more "constructive" in a work environment. Consider also that the expression "making waves" is generally used in a negative sense.

Thus whether it is better to make waves or calm waves depends on what you are trying to achieve. Let us look at **sound waves.** Is sound objective or subjective? Or as the cliché goes: If a tree falls in the forest and nobody is there to hear it, will it make a sound? If you hold a briefing and nobody is there to hear you, does your speech have meaning? The transmission of sound requires a medium, because if there is nothing to compress and expand there can be no sound. Let's say that you have an audience, but they don't *want* to listen. So they hear only what they want to hear and not what is actually being said. This is a communication problem. The so-called grapevine is an example of how sound travels like a wave even to those who didn't hear the original speaker. The reflection of sound is called an **echo**. If the surfaces reflecting the sound are too reflective, however, the sound becomes garbled and induces multiple reflections called **reverberations**. When this happens you may not hear the sound as it was originally intended. This is what propagates the transmission of rumors.

Mirrors are poor **absorbers** but good **reflectors**. Rough surfaces are better absorbers but poorer reflectors. It is difficult to be a good absorber and a good reflector at the same time. This concept, too, can be related to communication. Although you can be both a good transmitter and a good receiver of information by thinking about what you want to say before you say it, and ensuring that you really listen to what is being said when your team comes to you with their concerns, you cannot be a good transmitter and a good receiver precisely at the same time. It is only possible to focus on one issue at a time whether transmitting or receiving. Likewise, multi-tasking which has become increasingly popular, is an idea that should be rethought. Are employees really more efficient when they are forced to focus on several issues simultaneously? Might it be better if they were allowed to finish one task before being asked to perform another?

Consider also how aberration affects communication. In physics, **aberration** is the distortion of an image produced by a lens or system of lenses. No lens provides a perfect image. Aberration can be minimized by combining lenses in certain ways. For this reason most optical instruments use compound lenses, each consisting of several simple lenses instead of a single lens. In the workplace, if you want a clear and truthful view of your policies, you must involve others and ask for their views (you must look at the situation through different lenses), because your view alone may be distorted by a number of factors. This concept relates to **parallax**, or the apparent change in position of an object resulting from a change in the viewer's position. Due to the error of parallax, what you see from your position may not be what is actually there. To get a true image, objects must be viewed from a true position. If you view your team's performance from the outside but don't really experience it firsthand, your opinion of what is happening may be invalid simply because of your position. This can also be thought of as **frame of reference**, or a vantage point with respect to which an object may be described. Depending on where you stand, your frame of reference will differ from somebody else's. A team leader or manager, for example, may not see what the employees see because he is literally not in the fray on a daily basis and may therefore make false assumptions about the work environment.

WHAT DO YOU OWE YOUR TEAM?

You should now have gained an understanding of ways to Lead with Science, the strengths and the pitfalls. It is now appropriate to ask what you really owe your team and what your team owes you outside of what is stated in your written contract. Or do you owe each other nothing but eight hours of work and a paycheck? When you evaluate your team members, what do you wish to achieve and how will you use the evaluations to further your goals? Is your purpose to inspire employees to become more efficient? Although motivation may be our strongest driving force, to remain hungry and receptive to motivation the employee must realize the value of the task he or she is attempting to accomplish. In other words, the evaluation must make him or her feel good about working. The work must matter, the results must matter, and they must matter in the near future. If "above standard" on an evaluation promises a pay raise five years from now, it will most likely not serve as a good motivator. Likewise, "[w]aiting to praise or reprimand an employee for a specific behavior at a semi-annual performance review . . . will have a marginal impact on performance . . . [Y]early performance appraisals, annual recognition dinners, quarterly bonuses, and employee of the month contests have little or no impact on organizational performance."[10]

Rewards must also be large enough to make a difference. They must be fair. A year-end bonus that is given only to those who have worked for the company at least ten years will create negative attitudes for those who worked just as hard in the last year, but only have three years of service with the company. Which is fair: Should a bonus be a percentage of your salary, or should it be equal for everybody? This and other questions must be answered and considered carefully before proceeding. The consequences of your actions must also be considered, and whether they will help or hinder the situation.

Let's continue by looking at how to critique performance in order to increase motivation, and how to identify factors that can sabotage your best intentions when giving your employees their yearly evaluations.

CONSTRUCTIVE CRITICISM? OH YEAH?!

Critique increases motivation, *but only* if the critique is fair and the person critiqued understands its value. For the record, a critique is "a critical and unbiased analysis," which is not the same as *criticism*. Know the difference. You can give constructive critique but not constructive criticism. Criticism is by nature destructive. Although critique may be unpleasant and invite the possibility of an attack on your person, when allowed to critique widely we eliminate much subjective thought. When critiquing an employee's performance, for the critique to have meaning you must first ensure that the employee welcomes your input and is in a position to receive it. If you think you can change a person or a person's behavior without his or her approval, place yourself in the position of the person critiqued and the answer will immediately become clear. Furthermore, for a critique to be valid it must account for the verified results of a former critique; it must *correspond* with the former critique.

Here is an example: Joe's annual evaluation is due. The company has printed forms for this purpose, and you check the appropriate boxes for below standard, standard, and above standard performance for the different work duties. You call Joe into the office, give him a copy of the evaluation, and ask him to read and sign it. But Joe is unhappy despite the fact that you have given him mostly high marks. You have the sense to ask why, and Joe explains that this year's evaluation does not correspond with last year's evaluation. Last year another supervisor evaluated

Joe, and Joe now wants to know why you evaluated him as standard on ability to work with others, when the other supervisor gave him an above standard score in this particular area. You tell Joe that you have never had any complaints about him from his peers, but nobody in particular has complimented him either so you feel the standard mark fits. But Joe is still not happy and explains that last year nobody complained or complimented him either, yet the work went smoothly and he received an above standard on the evaluation. You admit that you have not looked at last year's evaluation, and that this year's evaluation is based on your experiences and not on the old boss' experiences. Joe is still unhappy. He is now telling you that an evaluation should not be subjective. If it is only up to your opinion, he says, it has little value because another leader will most certainly have a different opinion. And how can Joe make improvements to his performance if it is based on subjective opinion and not on objective fact?

How do you tackle this problem? You can start by asking whether the results of last year's evaluation have been fully verified, and how. What criteria did the last person use who evaluated Joe? If the criteria have changed or are subjective, will the old evaluation still be valid? Why, or why not? If the old and the new evaluations fail to correspond in the region where the results of the old evaluation have been fully verified, the old evaluation is invalid, the new evaluation is invalid, or both the old and the new evaluations are invalid. An evaluation that is invalid fails to accomplish its intent and is a waste of time.

As Joe noted, an evaluation must also be objective. What is objective? First, it should not be based on personal opinion of performance. In other words, if somebody else had made the same observations of a particular employee's performance, he should have given a similar critique. Second, it should not be based on whether or not you, the person administering the critique, like the person you are critiquing. Your mood on the particular day should not interfere. If you give the critique tomorrow, it should be the same as if you give it today. You must also base the critique on the actual performance that took place and not on what could have been. Third, the critique must be flexible to the degree that it fits the particular person, times, and circumstances that you are critiquing. It should not be taken out of context. Fourth, if the person receiving the critique does not agree, or at least accept it, it is worthless. A critique should not be an opportunity to voice your dissatisfaction with the person you are critiquing. For the employee to accept the critique, it is essential that the person administering the critique is an authority on the subject. If the person critiqued does not believe that you know what you are talking about, the critique will have little meaning. The fact that you are wearing a team leader patch does not alone qualify you to give an effective and acceptable critique.

Furthermore, a critique does not need to include every single area of performance. Rather, choose one or two points that are current at the moment. Remember to include the positive aspects of the employee's performance and not just the areas that need improvement. Finally, if the critique does not serve the intended purpose: to profit the person receiving the critique, it has failed. The person critiqued must thus know how to capitalize on the things covered in the critique. When identifying strengths and weaknesses, you must also provide a satisfactory explanation of how you reached your assessment. When identifying weaknesses, you must provide a specific way to overcome them. Disciplinary action, like critique, is useless unless it leads you a step closer to your objective. If you need to discipline a worker, how can you ensure that the discipline is constructive and more than a way for you to vent your feelings? How do you tailor it to benefit the needs of your organization? When you make suggestions for improvement, which is more important and why: the end result or how the employee goes about achieving it?

THE END OR THE MEANS?

The end is more important than the means, at least at a civilian place of employment. This is one reason why it is counterproductive to evaluate a person on whether or not he or she used the customer's name in conversation, smiled at the customer, or finished the conversation with, "Thank you for calling (enter your company's name here)." If whatever the employee did resulted in customer satisfaction, then exactly what he did is important only to him and not to the supervisor or others, because if they were to do the exact same thing it may not prove as effective because it would not play to their natural talents. When following a predetermined script such as, "Thank you for calling . . ." or, "How may I help you?" or using the customer's name at least twice, or making at least three attempts to sell a product, we tend not to hear the customer, but become absorbed only in following the script for fear that we may be monitored and *criticized*. This kind of monitoring and criticism is meaningless and misses the point, because the employee would be evaluated on how well he or she follows the script and not on how well he or she treats the customer. He would thus be evaluated on the means and not the end.

One company recently implemented a quality assurance program that required team leaders to observe and evaluate the employees during their performance. One leader confessed that he had to evaluate each employee twice during the month and had more than fifty employees to evaluate. First, if you have to produce a forced evaluation this often it is an indication that you don't know the people on your team. And if you don't know your people, you are not fit to be their leader. Second, just about all of the employees were receiving high marks in all areas but were offered little specific input. In other words, the team leader wrote the evaluation only because there was pressure from above, and not because he considered it an important part of the operation. If you are a team leader evaluating or rating an employee and you cannot offer specific input, it may be tempting to use an "average" rating. Try to avoid this temptation. Do not rate on a scale from one to five, for example, because it would tempt you to choose "three." The idea is that we are either happy or not. Choosing the average score is a copout. You are in fact saying that you are not completely happy with the employee, but you are not unhappy either. In other words, you can get by with the status quo, which means that there is really no motivation to improve. So what do we do? We get by.

The end is thus more important than the means, because the means must always be judged in relation to the end they serve. If the end is not achieved, the procedure of going through an evaluation process is useless. Before implementing a quality assurance program, you must first define the end objective: What are you trying to achieve? If you are trying to achieve better workers (whatever that means) but the evaluation serves to antagonize the workers, then you have not achieved the end objective. If the workers accept the evaluation but do not change as a result, you have not achieved the end objective. To reiterate: For people to change, they must want to change. How do you know if you will reach the end objective before you have wasted your time? A good place to start is by asking those affected: the workers. If they take negatively to your ideas, you might want to proceed cautiously.

EVALUATING THE LEADER

    Just as an evaluation done by the team leader must be precise with clearly defined objectives to have meaning, so must an evaluation done by the employees. When I asked my coworkers what qualities they would like to see in a team leader, their answers were weighted toward following through on commitments and promises, offering help even if no help is needed, and asking for opinions before implementing new rules. As an employee, if you are offered a questionnaire about how the leadership is doing, simply checking a box that says that the manager recognizes excellence, tells us nothing of value about the leadership. You need to take it a step further and ask *how*. Then give a specific example. If you cannot give a specific example of how the team leader stresses teamwork or holds people accountable for their actions, he or she will fail to identify with the critique and the critique will be meaningless; it will be nothing but an exercise in futility and a waste of time.

    By contrast, a well conducted team leader/manager evaluation done by the employees will give the leadership the ability to extract information that can be used to make the company more productive. To act on the information, the team leaders must also have their manager's blessing; they must be allowed to do the job that has been delegated to them. To score well on an evaluation as a team leader, you must understand and have insight into the following:

1. **For whom you are working.** There is only one correct answer. I will give you a hint: It is in your title. The team leader is serving the team. You are not serving the customer, the company, or the manager. You are serving the team. Period. In other words, if you answer that you are working for the company, the team, management, your paycheck, and the customer, it would be a cosmic clause statement that dilutes the role of the leader and indicates that you don't have a clear understanding of what it means to be a team leader. Choose one of the above, not all. The team leader does not wear many hats, as some would have us believe. The team leader has only one responsibility: his team. It is thus important that you understand your role. Being a leader is not a prerequisite for becoming a manager or a business executive. Some would have us believe that it is, but there is really very little practical connection. The reverse is also true. Team leaders and company managers play distinctly different roles. This concept holds true for many jobs within the company. There is not necessarily a "ladder" within the team or company that each employee must climb. The duties that need to be performed require different talents, and one job function does not naturally lead to another. (Must a pilot be a flight attendant before he or she can be a pilot? Must an author write children's books before he or she can write for adults? Of course not. The occupations are different and one is not a steppingstone for the other.) Some individuals are, of course, good at performing several functions, but it should not be assumed that everybody can be trained to do so successfully or is interested in being trained for a new position for that matter. An outstanding

leader must also do more than what is naturally expected of him. If the company places a statement on the wall that reads, "What have you done today that made the customer smile?" before expecting results from the employees, the leader might want to ask himself what he has done today that made an employee smile. Be specific. Simply saying that you are fair and listen to suggestions coming from your team is not precise enough. Additionally, just as airline customers expect to be delivered to their destination safely, being fair and listening to suggestions sort of comes with your position and doesn't add any additional value to your score.

2. **For whom your team is working.** Again, there is only one correct answer. I will give you a hint: Your team (if it is well-run and efficient) does NOT work for the team leader, the company, or the customer. All of these answers are wrong. The team is serving itself. Customer service is a byproduct of a well-run team. This concept lies at the heart of team leadership. When you select your team, you must select people who want to work with each other. As already explored, randomly grouping any number of people together does not make a team. When people want to work together, they will help each other and further contribute to the cohesiveness of the team. Without team cohesiveness you don't have a team; each worker will be working alone. As a result, customer service will suffer.

3. **The misuse and abuse of the saying, "There is no I in team."** As we have already explored, the team is built around the "I" concept.

Identity, for example, involves more than wearing the uniform or mouthing a slogan. The "selfish" needs of the team members must be satisfied before the needs of the customer can be satisfied. Feed the team first to establish a sense of pride and ownership. The members of the team must feel their successes regularly and know that their opinions matter. The team's vision must also be stated clearly, agreed upon by the members, and achievable within a reasonable time. "To become the world's greatest" is in a practical sense as useless as "to become a millionaire" or "to understand the meaning of life." Remember that your team could do a better job IF they wanted to. The trick is not making them do a better job, but identifying the factors that will make them WANT to do a better job.

Furthermore, the leader should be an ally and not a troublemaker. Perceived dishonesty is just as bad as true dishonesty. At one corporation, one of the leaders revealed that he had received only two out of five possible points for honesty on an evaluation done by the workers, and it puzzled him. At the same corporation, one of the managers realized that he must work on improving the relationship between the team and the leadership. It took him forty-five minutes to walk from one end of the hallway to the other, because he could not take a step without being stopped by frustrated workers whose team leaders had failed to follow up on their concerns.

There is little incentive for employees to be committed to the goals of an organization that makes no reciprocal commitment to the employees. Getting out of the office and mingling with the employees can be a simple solution to common trust problems. However, one must also ensure that the employees understand the reason for the manager or team leader getting out of the office. If he appears out of character by doing so, he risks losing trust rather than gaining it. Ask: How should the manager or team leader be visible? In the shadows? In the break room? In the work area? Why? Where should he not be? Employees with customer contact are often told that they are in a fishbowl; that they should be aware of their behavior because the customers are constantly watching. This idea applies also to the leader. The difference is that he is on stage for those he leads. Every move you make is observed and evaluated by your employees and contributes to the attitudes they form about you and the job.

When striving to score well on an evaluation done by the employees the leader should keep in mind that:

1. Most people don't like change, never have, and never will. This is the truth! Forcing change when not warranted ALWAYS has a negative outcome.

2. Most people respond much better if you ask them what they want rather than tell them what they should want.

3. Most people are not lazy and don't inherently dislike work. But a successful team leader/team relationship, just as a successful marriage, requires constant reinforcement.

Now, then, it is the employee's turn. If you are an employee, here are some suggestions that might help you answer questions that might appear on an evaluation you are asked to write about your team leader's performance. If you cannot answer all of these questions by giving specific examples, you need to slow down, backtrack, or take a good look at the full picture and question whether your assumptions are really valid.

MY TEAM LEADER

1. **Cares about whether or not I am happy at work and makes an effort to find out what makes me tick.** When you answer this question, rather than simply placing an X in the "yes" or "no" box, state what your team leader has done to indicate that he cares about your satisfaction. For example, has he or she recently asked what you need to feel job satisfaction? If he or she doesn't care about you, you will feel as though you are just a number among others without specific value. When you have no value, you will not put forth the effort to do a good job.

2. **Asks my opinion about issues that affect me and makes an attempt to accommodate my views.** Has your supervisor asked your opinion regarding issues that affect you; for example, with whom you would like to work, in which area you would like to work (if applicable), whether you have the equipment you need to do your job efficiently, and what in particular can be done to make you feel more joy about coming to work? How important is it that he or she implements your suggestions? Or is it good enough if the leader says, "Yes, I hear you and I agree, but there is nothing I can do about it!" A leader must work for his people's cause. If the arguments presented by the employees are not valid, they still need to be discussed until the leader and the employees reach common ground.

3. **Acknowledges my efforts and rewards me for my work when warranted.** When answering this question, keep in mind that proper recognition generally involves more than a "good job yesterday." There must be some form of concrete reward. For example, if employee A finishes a job faster than employee B, then employee A should be personally rewarded (for example, with a break), and not "punished" by being asked to work more than employee B, in which case the supervisor would in effect be rewarding the slackers.

4. **Gives suggestions for how I might improve my performance.** As discussed previously, for feedback to be constructive problems must first be agreed upon between team leader and employee. If the supervisor were required to wear a shirt at work with a sign on the back that read, "How is my leadership? Call 1-800- . . ." would he think it a good idea? Even if he or she possesses many good leadership qualities, my guess is that he would not welcome this idea because there is always somebody who is having a bad day and cannot wait to take advantage of the opportunity. For an evaluation to be constructive, both parties involved must agree on the problem area and be allowed to confront each other and discuss it. Anonymous evaluations where the subject has no way of elaborating, asking for clarification, defending himself, etc. will never go over well with the person evaluated, and are in principle always wrong even if the results of the evaluation turn out to be outstanding.

5. Is available when I need him or her. There are two sides to consider here: A team leader who gets involved where he is not needed is worse than one who does not get involved at all. A team leader who is visible in the operation does not necessarily ensure that the employees' needs are met.

6. Has character and creates an impression of integrity and trust. Many team leaders likely perform their jobs with integrity; they are basically good people. However, do they have the education and drive to be good leaders and not just good people? You may trust your team leader as far as "yes, I feel safe coming to work." But do you trust him or her as far as "will he or she stand up for me if I make a mistake?"

7. Enforces compliance with established procedures. Sometimes leaders break the rules, just like employees do when they think they can get away with it and when it helps make their jobs easier. If this happens often, consider whether it might be the rules that need an overhaul and not the team leaders. If this is the case, is the team leader willing to rewrite the rules so that they affect everybody equally?

8. Encourages new ideas and is willing to change when applicable. As we have seen, change is not necessarily beneficial and is therefore not necessarily something that should be encouraged. In fact, unneeded change creates stress and sabotages team spirit and work ethics. The team leader will be more successful if he or she asks the employees directly what would help them do a better job.

Sometimes we feel there is an artificial need to change. In other words, the need is not real. But since things are not going well, we need to do something about it so that we can prove to our superiors that we have at least addressed the issue. Before implementing the change, did the team leader clearly state why the change was needed and did he or she evaluate it afterward to determine to what extent the change helped fix the problem? A manager at one company admitted to me in private that he forced an unwelcome change that did not improve efficiency, because he had to demonstrate to his superiors that he had made an attempt to improve efficiency or face demotion.

As an alternative when evaluating your team leader, focus only on one issue rather than several and explain how the leader excels or fails on this particular issue. Although we would like to think that the leader should be assertive, friendly, a good listener, flexible, and knowledgeable all at once, does he really need to know every aspect of the operation? Is well-rounded always better than specialist? Why, or why not? Although the team as a whole should have the capacity to perform the entire job, each individual on the team does not need this capacity. Similarly, the leader can be specialized in a particular area of the operation and rely on the support of the team in areas where he is not a specialist. Those who put together evaluations or surveys are likely to fall into the brainstorming trap and list as much as possible rather than settling for a few particular points. The problem is that few people are able to excel at fifteen different qualities. If a particular leader would score strongly in just one area, he might be rated "exceptional" by those employees who have a need for this particular leadership quality. But this is better than being rated "mediocre" in all fifteen areas. If you can specialize in one talent or quality, you have a better chance of succeeding in leadership than if you are a "jack of all trades." Just as individual team member skills and methods differ and *should* differ, so do individual leadership skills and methods.

Another thing to keep in mind when evaluating your team leader is that people with similar personalities and outlooks on life may get along better with each other than those with different personalities and outlooks, and some employees may therefore give the team leader a higher rating than others. In this sense, the team leader evaluation can become subjective rather than objective or scientific. This does not in itself mean that one person's evaluation is more correct than another's; it only means that a particular leader is a better "pitcher" for you than for somebody else. This is yet a reason why you should give specific examples when answering the questions on the evaluation and avoid simple "yes" or "no" answers, or worse, give the team leader a three on a scale of five. Keep in mind that under different circumstances, in a different company, with a different mission, or with a different team, the score might have been different, too.

Finally, for a team leader/supervisor evaluation to have meaning, the team leader must listen to what the employees are really saying on the evaluation. Written surveys with specific questions and multiple choice answers ranging from dislike to like are not accurate, because these sorts of answers are void of meaning and therefore difficult to compile into something meaningful. Answers need to be qualified with explanations or definitions if we are to ensure that everybody really understands what is being said. As an alternative, the team leader might want to listen in causally to what is being said in the break room and behind the scenes to get an idea of how the employees really think and feel. This approach will take a bit more work or dedication than simply handing out a survey, but it can be used as a tool for avoiding the application of a generic approach that will apply to nobody in particular when trying to fix problems. Remember that a great part of the leader's success has to do with how the team perceives him or her.

CAN YOU HEAR THE TALK?

No leadership book would be complete without mentioning the importance of proper communication. The ability to draw from the resourcefulness of your team can help you catch mistakes before they become morale destroyers. Good resource management emphasizes communication and the spread of information.

The person transmitting the message must demonstrate that he believes in the message he is sending. Great leaders have charisma that gives them the power to manipulate people's emotions. As Adolf Hitler said, "I know that fewer people are won over by the written word than by the spoken word, and that every great movement on this earth owes its growth to great speakers and not to great writers."[11] I am not asking that you approve of Adolf Hitler, but rather that you recognize that there is some truth to this statement. Great leaders can make you see logic where there is no truth. Great leaders can control the masses, but they can also abuse their power. Thus the receiver carries part of the responsibility for deciphering the message. A team leader that I know held a twenty-minute briefing, which was actually a twenty-minute one-man show. The dynamics of his delivery left no doubt in my mind that he believed strongly in the message and, after the lecture, I wanted to applaud him. But as I allowed the experience to settle, I discovered that what had kept me so captivated was not the message, but his *conviction* in the message. In the end, there were few things he had said that I actually agreed with.

Although the leader must be passionate and committed to his cause if he is to inspire others to follow, and although his speech might demonstrate passion, a speech alone does not necessarily demonstrate commitment. Equally important, even if the leader is passionate and committed, he does not necessarily know the steps required to reach the goal or vision. Simply saying that you are committed to running the greatest business in the world will not allow you to accomplish this goal, if you cannot also list the required steps and follow through on your commitment.

Communication is an active process that requires participation. Communication involves listening and understanding the other person's perceptions, which requires interaction between the speaker and the listener. Active listeners ask questions rather than find something to argue about; they paraphrase the information to increase their understanding of what is being said. Passive listeners have already decided beforehand what they want to hear and can therefore not listen to what is really being said.

Leaders should ask questions to draw information from the employees. But questions intended to test an employee's knowledge, although valuable in certain other situations, have no place in communication. Effective questions are formed by asking what, where, how, and why. Listen with the intent to explore the answer. To avoid confusion, make questions concise and ask only one thing at a time. Be sensible but also require that others give you a chance. When communicating, avoid questions that:

1. Are open-ended: "Do you have any questions?" The answer to an open-ended question is not likely to give you much new insight. It is simply too easy for the employee to say "no."

2. Are complex, require the person to solve a puzzle, or have a catch. This is not a test of who is smarter. The purpose of asking questions is not to quiz the employee on his or her knowledge, but to gain information. Moreover, employees are not mind readers. Contribute with information when you sense that an employee doesn't know where you are headed.

3. Cover everything: "What would you do to increase customer service?" It is better to ask a question that pertains to a particular situation: "When Mrs. Smith complained about the extra fee, name one thing you think we could have done that would have alleviated customer aggravation."

4. Give you a choice of this or that: "Should you greet the customer by first name or last name?" These sorts of questions are invalid because they force the person to make a choice even if both options are incorrect (or correct for that matter). Perhaps the customer prefers anonymity and doesn't want to be greeted by name at all.

5. Lead the employee to always answer "yes." For example: "Do you want a career that rewards you for your achievements?" Or, "Do you want to make six figures a year?" Well, duh, who wouldn't? Employees, beware! These types of questions usually

have a hidden agenda. Think pyramid scheme. How much you earn in these types of jobs depends strictly on commission or how many incredibly long hours you work for peanuts. These sorts of jobs will make all but a tiny minority of top performers work themselves into the ground and lose everything, their money as well as their dignity. How do you guard against this type of manipulative behavior? You define by asking, What type of career? What types of rewards are we talking about? How are they distributed and in what amount? What kind of achievement does it take to earn a reward?

Answering questions posed by your team may seem easy particularly if you know the answer, but there is an art here as well:

1. Make sure you fully understand what is being asked and avoid mechanical answers. If in doubt, answer the question by asking another question along the same lines. This may lead the employee to answer his own question.

2. Look for a response when you have answered the question. If the employee seems confused, quiet, or indifferent, you might need to elaborate on your answer.

3. When an employee confronts you with a problem, ask a question that starts with "why" to trigger his thinking process. He may now find the solution himself. When we derive a solution through our own reasoning, we will remember it better and give it greater approval.

4. Avoid yes or no answers. By giving a more thorough answer, you ensure that you really answer what is being asked.

5. It has been said that there are no dumb questions . . . only dumb people. Well, there are in fact both dumb questions and dumb people. But when somebody asks a dumb question, don't ridicule him or her or tell him it is a "no-brainer." The purpose is to gain information and not to test an employee's intelligence. If you sense that an employee is afraid to ask but burns with a desire to know, be generous and take the first step by suggesting an answer or solution to a perceived problem.

Asking and answering questions also requires that you listen to what your team is really saying. Do you listen to everybody on your team, or do you listen more to the people you particularly like; to those who squeal the loudest; or to those who make an effort to seek you out? Do you ask your employees to clarify questions that you don't understand fully? If you don't know the correct answer, do you make an effort to find it? Do you let others finish speaking without interrupting, or do you "put words in their mouth?" If somebody is upset, they might just have a need to vent and not a need to argue. Are you honest and able to present and accept the facts, or do you push others to accept your values? Give an example. Do you know where you stand? Do you make your actions match your words? Sending mixed messages is detrimental to effective communication. Do you say a definite yes or no when you mean to say a definite yes or no? Do you think about what you want to say before you say it, so that you can say exactly what you want to say?

Furthermore, when conveying a new idea to your team, their attitudes may indicate resistance, passivity, or an unwillingness to comply. Barriers to communication include:

1. Lack of common background experiences. Understanding the team's background helps you determine the approach you should take when communicating.

2. Lack of commitment or lack of trust. How the transmitter and the receiver of the message feel during the exchange has an impact on how the message is perceived.

3. Physical and mental discomfort. When either the transmitter or the receiver is grouchy, ill, or uncomfortable, the message may not be transmitted or received as intended, or may not be received at all. A friend of mine once told me, "If it ain't right at home, it ain't right at work either."

4. Argumentation. Recognize an invitation to argue and avoid it. Consider how your team will view you if you accept an argument openly. Note that argumentation is not synonymous with debate or discussion.

Now that you know how to ask and answer questions, can you hear the talk? Conflicts are not necessarily bad but become so when you fail to understand the essential issue. A conflict that is handled properly will increase your confidence and deepen your thinking. Most managers say they have an "open door policy," yet many employees don't feel they can take advantage of it, because whenever they come with an issue to discuss it is immediately shot down. They are even interrupted when presenting it because the manager has already made up his mind. So, in fact, having an open door policy does not automatically make the manager more "approachable" even if he is "available." If people are uncomfortable talking with you, it will not matter how "open" your door is, they will stop coming to you with suggestions or ideas; they will stop asking for your help; they will bypass you on the chain of command when something needs to get done. If you listen an awful lot but never take what is said to heart, people will begin to see the futility of the situation and stop wasting their time on you.

All sources of information are valuable, but few are as valuable as the person who uses his knowledge to guide others. Do not accept a challenge to prove a point. Keep sensitive issues behind closed doors and remember that people are people first before they are agents, workers, or employees. When times are bad it is fruitless to remind your team that they should be happy they have a job at all. People have emotions and when they are upset, they are not likely to respond to what you have to say. People don't listen or change when they are threatened or forced to do so. You must invite them in and meet them halfway. The transmitter must be ready, willing, and able to communicate the message. The receiver must be ready, willing, and able to receive the message. If we are concerned only with ourselves, we will say only what we want to say and hear only what we want to hear. Whether or not the wheel that squeaks gets the grease or silence is golden is a matter of timing. Whether or not a quiet person is a good or bad communicator is a matter of timing. The wheel turns one way, but it also turns the other way. Time a message right by asking, "Which way is the wheel turning?"

Now that you know something about communication, the final test is your ability to communicate the whole truth. If an employee asks about his future with the company and you give him a vague answer like, "There are opportunities for growth and development," what has he or she learned? Absolutely nothing! When the truth is spoken, it challenges people to get involved and creates commitment and team spirit. Withholding the truth creates insecurity. Lack of truthful communication challenges the workers to find the information through their own reasoning—through rumors. Rumors, faulty information, and worry steal energy from the workforce. Thus when you share information or discuss new policies with your people, state the truth, all of it. If you withhold certain facts, you will be perceived as unreliable and dishonest. Bad news when told with sincerity and clear-sightedness will be taken in stride by the workers. It has been said that if you try to sit on two chairs at the same time, you will most likely fall in-between. Know on which chair you are sitting and face the truth with courage and honor. It is your responsibility as a leader to see and communicate things the way they are, and not the way you wish them to be.

A final warning: When communicating, don't put the buggy before the horse. When my shooting instructor was teaching me about the handgun, he had me dry-fire it a few times. Then he loaded the gun, handed it to me, and said, "If you pull the trigger now, the gun will fire." My finger tightened on the trigger and I broke out in a cold sweat when I realized how close I had come to firing the gun inside my home. *Pull now!* was all I had heard because these were the action words. If he had put the horse before the buggy instead of the other way around, he would have said, "Put the gun down, it is loaded," and then said, "If you were to pull the trigger now that the gun is loaded, the gun would fire."

So are the best leaders born or made? I don't know. I will let you decide.

NOTES

¹The author challenges the reader to consider to what extent this statement is true. Is science necessarily logic and steadfast? Has there ever been a time when we have proven a scientific principle false, perhaps many hundred years after its discovery?

²See Francis Bacon, Wikiquote, http://en.wikiquote.org/wiki/Knowledge.

³Nassir Ghaemi, *A First-Rate Madness: Uncovering the Links Between Leadership and Mental Illness* (New York, NY: Penguin Press, 2011), Kindle Edition.

⁴Marcus Buckingham and Curt Coffman, *First, Break All the Rules: What the World's Greatest Managers Do Differently* (New York, NY: Simon & Schuster, 1999), 172- 173.

⁵Ibid., 61-62.

⁶Ibid., 173.

⁷Ibid., 256.

⁸Supposedly said by Petronius Arbiter in the days of ancient Rome; although, it is disputed if he actually said this. See Richard A. Clarke, *Your Government Failed You: Breaking the Cycle of National Security Disasters* (New York, NY: HarperCollins Publishers, 2008), 205.

⁹See Paul G. Hewitt, *Conceptual Physics* (Glenview, IL: Scott, Foresman and Company, 1989), or any other book on elementary physics for further definition and information about the terms used here.

¹⁰Kitty Campbell, "Influence Employees the Right Way," *All Business* (May 1, 2002),

http://www.allbusiness.com/human-resources/workforce-management/209349-1.html.
    [11]Adolf Hitler, *Mein Kampf* (Boring, OR: CPA Book Publisher, first published in 1939), 6.

About the Author

Martina Sprague has a Master of Arts Degree in Military History from Norwich University in Vermont. As a historian she is particularly interested in political and social factors that influence the decisions of "Great Men" and the actions of their subordinates. She has written numerous books about military and political/social history. For more information, please visit her Web site: www.modernfighter.com.

www.ingramcontent.com/pod-product-compliance
Lightning Source LLC
Chambersburg PA
CBHW071605170526
45166CB00003B/1002